FOCUS ON

GERMANY
AND THE GERMANS

ANITA GANERI

GLOUCESTER PRESS
London · New York · Toronto · Sydney

© Aladdin Books Ltd 1992

Designed and produced by
Aladdin Books Ltd
28 Percy Street
London W1P 9FF

First published in
Great Britain in 1992 by
Franklin Watts Ltd
96 Leonard Street
London EC2A 4RH

ISBN 0 7496 0990 7

A CIP catalogue record for this book is
available from the British Library.

Printed in Belgium

Design	David West Children's Book Design
Designer	Flick Killerby
Series Director	Bibby Whittaker
Editor	Jen Green
Picture research	Emma Krikler
Illustrators	David Burroughs
	David Russell
	Peter Kesteven

The author, Anita Ganeri, has an M.A. in
French, German and Hindi from
Cambridge. She has lived and worked in
both France and Germany and has written
numerous children's books.

The consultant, Antony Mason, has an
M.A. in French and German from Oxford.
He has lived and worked in Germany, and
now writes and edits books for children.

INTRODUCTION

Germany is a large country situated at the
very centre of Europe. It is one of the
world's wealthiest nations, and the goods
it produces are popular all over the world.
Many famous artists, philosophers and
scientists are German. As a nation,
Germans are an industrious, energetic
people, with a love of both work and play.
Germany is a land of varied scenery, with
coastline and flat plains, river valleys,
hilly uplands, forests and mountains. This
book offers an insight into Germany and
the German people, and includes
information about geography, language
and literature, science and maths, history
and the arts. The key below shows how
these subjects are divided up.

Geography
The symbol of the planet Earth
indicates where
geographical facts and
activities are examined
in the book. These
sections include a summary
of the mineral resources
of Germany.

Language and literature
An open book is the sign for
activities and information
about language and literature.
These sections explore some of
the many great works of
literature that have been
produced by German writers.

Science, technology and maths

The microscope symbol shows where a science or maths subject is included. If the symbol is tinted green, it signals an environmental issue. German scientists have pioneered many breakthroughs. Germany's natural history is also explored in these sections.

History

The sign of the scroll and hourglass indicates where historical information is given. These sections look at key figures and events in German history, and their influence today.

Social history

The symbol of the family shows where information about social history is given. These sections provide an insight into the German way of life today, as well as describing religious beliefs, traditional festivals and customs.

Arts, crafts and music

The symbol showing a sheet of music and art tools signals where activities and information on arts, crafts or music are included. Germany has produced many famous composers and artists, some of whom are described in this book.

CONTENTS

INFLUENCE AND PRESENCE

Germany is one of the most influential countries in Europe, and one of the world's major economic powers. In 1871 the country was unified from a number of smaller states. But Germany's history has not always followed a smooth path. After World War II, Germany was divided again, into East and West. It was only reunified in 1990. The new *Bundesrepublik Deutschland* (Federal Republic of Germany) covers an area of about 357,000 square kilometres. It is a densely populated country, home to a population of nearly 79 million inhabitants.

Denmark

Poland

Netherlands

Germany

Belgium

Luxembourg

Czechoslovakia

France

Liechtenstein

Hungary

Switzerland

Austria

Italy

■ Germany

▨ German-speaking countries

□ German-speaking regions

High and Low German

German is the official language of Germany, Austria and Liechtenstein, and is spoken in parts of Belgium, Switzerland and Italy (above). It belongs to the same language group as English and Dutch. The official language spoken in Germany today is known as High German. It was first standardised by monks in the 1100s. A dialect, called Low German, is also spoken in the north. Many other parts of Germany also have their own regional dialects.

Musical Germany

Some of the world's greatest musicians and composers have come from Germany. They include Bach, Handel, Beethoven, Mendelssohn, Schumann and Wagner. George Frideric Handel (below) was born in Germany but composed his most famous work, *Messiah*, in England.

Handel
1685-1759

The eagle is the best known symbol of Germany. It has been used in Germany since the 1st century AD, when it appeared on the Roman standard. The German flag (top left) is a tricolour of black, red and gold. These were the colours of the Weimar Republic (see page 8).

Living standards

Germans enjoy a high standard of living. Before reunification, people in West Germany had more money, and better clothes, cars and shops than East Germans. These goods are now available to East Germans. Many have lost their jobs in the east, however, and cannot afford them.

Like Leipzig (above), many cities in the former East Germany contain old-fashioned buildings in need of repair. Frankfurt (left) in the former West Germany, is a bustling city with many modern buildings.

Between 1949 and 1990 Germany was divided into two parts. West Germany (FDR) was a modern, prosperous part of Europe. East Germany (GDR) was one of the wealthiest Communist countries, but still lagged well behind its neighbour in economic development. The two halves of Germany were officially reunited on 3 October, 1990.

Germany has one of the strongest economies in the world. After World War II, West Germany quickly built its economy back up. The East German economy was strictly controlled by the Communist government. The two countries merged economies in 1990.

Bach
1685-1750

Johann Sebastian Bach (left) was the greatest composer of Baroque music. He lived in Leipzig, and was also an accomplished organist. The world-famous Berlin Philharmonic orchestra (right) continues Germany's musical tradition today.

The Berlin Philharmonic

Rocket science

Wernher von Braun (1912-1977) was a leading rocket scientist. He headed the rocket team that built the V-2 missile, used during World War II. Von Braun was sent to America in 1945 and became a US citizen. He helped to develop the Saturn V rocket which put American astronauts on the Moon.

EARLY HISTORY

Two thousand years ago, the map of western Europe was dominated by the Roman Empire. But in the 1st century BC, Germany was invaded by tribes from northern Europe who halted the Roman advance. The Franks were the most powerful of these tribes. Under Charlemagne, the kingdom of the Franks included Germany, France and northern Italy. After Charlemagne's death, Germany became part of the Holy Roman Empire. This empire, made up of separate kingdoms and principalities, was dominated from 1438 to 1806 by the powerful Hapsburg family of Austria.

During the 16th century, a German monk called Martin Luther brought conflict to the Holy Roman Empire. In 1517 Luther began to attack the teachings and practices of the powerful Roman Catholic Church. His movement was called the Reformation and his followers, Protestants. Germany divided into Protestant and Catholic states. Their rivalry led to the Thirty Years' War (1618-1648), which left Germany in ruins.

Following the war, the state of Prussia rose to become the strongest in Germany. Its capital was in Berlin. Prussia's most successful king was Frederick II (the Great) who ruled from 1740 to 1786. He challenged the power of the Hapsburgs by fighting two wars with Austria.

**Martin Luther
(1483-1546)**

Printing and script

In the 1450s, Johann Gutenberg (right), from Mainz, invented the printing press. The printing process he developed was used throughout Europe for the next 350 years. Among Gutenberg's first printed works was a bible, which became known as the Gutenberg Bible.

The Gutenberg Bible was printed in Gothic script (below). This script was used to print some German newspapers until recently. Try writing your name in Gothic script, using a calligraphy pen.

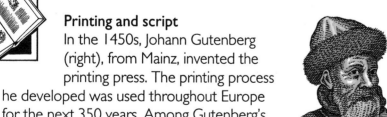

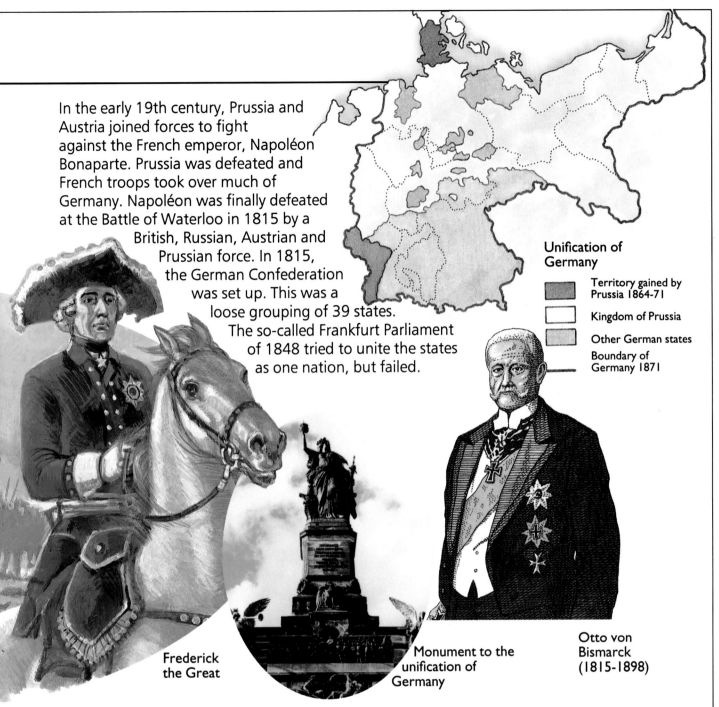

In the early 19th century, Prussia and Austria joined forces to fight against the French emperor, Napoléon Bonaparte. Prussia was defeated and French troops took over much of Germany. Napoléon was finally defeated at the Battle of Waterloo in 1815 by a British, Russian, Austrian and Prussian force. In 1815, the German Confederation was set up. This was a loose grouping of 39 states. The so-called Frankfurt Parliament of 1848 tried to unite the states as one nation, but failed.

Unification of Germany

Territory gained by Prussia 1864-71

Kingdom of Prussia

Other German states

Boundary of Germany 1871

Frederick the Great

Monument to the unification of Germany

Otto von Bismarck (1815-1898)

In 1862, Otto von Bismarck became prime minister of Prussia. A brilliant politician, Bismarck vowed to use "iron and blood" to unite Germany under Prussia. He expanded Prussia's influence by fighting three short wars, against Denmark (1864) Austria (1866) and France (1870-1871). In 1871, Germany was unified, and the Prussian king, Wilhelm I, became the first emperor, or *Kaiser*. Bismarck became its first chancellor and the head of the government.

The German Empire quickly became very powerful in Europe. In 1888, Wilhelm II succeeded his father as *Kaiser*. He quarrelled with Bismarck, and forced him to resign in 1890. Then he tried to increase Germany's power and territory abroad, to the alarm of other European countries. Russia, France and Britain joined forces for protection. Austria and Italy sided with Germany. War between the two sides seemed more and more likely.

Wilhelm II

20TH CENTURY HISTORY

In 1914, the murder of the Austrian Crown Prince in Sarajevo in Bosnia triggered World War I. Millions of people were killed in the fighting, and Germany was eventually defeated. In the years after the war, inflation and unemployment led to unrest. All this paved the way for the rise of Adolf Hitler and the Nazi party in the 1930s. Hitler promised better things for the German people (*Volk*) at the expense of those he saw as inferior, such as Slavs and Jews. In 1939 Hitler invaded Poland, and World War II broke out. After the war, defeated Germany was divided among the Allies. It remained divided until 1990.

German soldiers in World War I

World War I

World War I ended in 1918, when Germany was defeated by the Allied forces of France, Britain, Russia, the United States and Italy. In the Treaty of Versailles signed after the war, the Allies imposed harsh penalties on Germany. Some saw these terms as likely to cause another war.

In 1919, Germany was declared a republic, known as the Weimar Republic. But the government was weak. In the 1920s inflation was so high that German money became almost worthless. The economy collapsed and many could not find jobs. The Nazi party took advantage of the confusion and unrest. In 1934, Adolf Hitler declared himself *Führer* (leader). His aim was to make Germany all powerful.

After World War II, Germany's capital city, Berlin, was stranded deep inside the zone occupied by the Soviet Union. The city was divided into four parts among the Allies. In August 1961, the East German government built a wall across it (above) to stop people escaping into the West.

Huge rallies were held in the city of Nuremberg, to show support for the Nazis. After World War II, Nazi leaders were put on trial there for war crimes. Many were sentenced to death.

World War II

In World War II (1939-1945) the Allied forces of Britain, France, the United States and the Soviet Union fought Germany, Italy and Japan. Millions perished in the war, which left German cities such as Aachen (right) in ruins. Germany surrendered in 1945 and was divided into four zones, controlled by the Allies (below). In 1949, the three western zones became West Germany. The eastern, Soviet-controlled zone became East Germany.

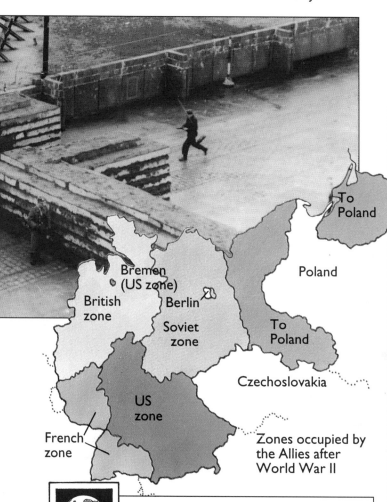

To Poland

Poland

Bremen (US zone)

British zone

Berlin

Soviet zone

To Poland

French zone

US zone

Czechoslovakia

Zones occupied by the Allies after World War II

A Jewish land

During World War II, about 6 million Jews were murdered in Nazi concentration camps. This was part of Hitler's plan to rid Germany of any people who were not pure Germans. In 1948, the state of Israel was created in the Middle East as a homeland to which Jews from all over the world could return.

DATES IN RECENT GERMAN HISTORY

1914-18 World War I
1919 Treaty of Versailles
Weimar Republic in Germany
1933 Adolf Hitler and the Nazis (National Socialist German Workers' Party) come to power.
1939-45 World War II
1949 Division of Germany into West Germany and Communist East Germany.
1953 The Soviet Union crushes a revolt in East Germany.
1955 East and West Germany are declared independent, and join opposing sides in the "Cold War" between the Soviet Union and the United States.
1961 The Berlin Wall is erected.
1973 East and West Germany sign a treaty which calls for closer relations between them. Both countries join the United Nations (UN).
1989 The Berlin Wall is knocked down. East German citizens are allowed to travel freely to West Germany.
1990 March: Free elections are held in East Germany, resulting in the end of Communist rule. October: Germany is reunified.

Prussian Victory Monument in Berlin

THE COUNTRY

Germany has a very varied landscape, ranging from the flat, fertile plains of the north to the central highlands and the great peaks of the Bavarian Alps in the south, which mark Germany's border with Austria. Most of Germany has mild summers, cool winters and moderate rainfall all year round. The coastlines in the north, and the Rhine Valley, usually enjoy milder weather than other parts of the country. There are picturesque river valleys and thick forests in south and central Germany.

Rivers
The Rhine (above) and the Elbe are the longest rivers which flow through Germany. The Rhine is a major waterway. The banks of the middle Rhine are lined with small towns and vineyards which make Germany's famous white wines (see page 16). Magnificent castles such as Burg Rheinfels (top left) were originally built to guard the river.

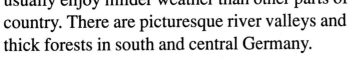

Baltic Sea

North Sea

Kiel •

Rügen Is

• Rostock

Lübeck •

• Hamburg

R Peene

R Weser

• Bremen

Lüneberg Heath

R Oder

NORTH GERMAN PLAIN

R Aller

R Havel

R Ems

Teutoburg Forest

Weser Hills

• Hanover

Berlin •

R Ruhr

Harz Mts

R Spree

• Düsseldorf

Rothaar Mts

• Kassel

Spree Forest

Cologne •

• Leipzig

• Aachen

CENTRAL HIGHLANDS

R Elbe

• Bonn

Thuringian Forest

R Saale

• Dresden

R Rhine

Ore Mountains

R Mosel

Wiesbaden •

• Frankfurt

• Mainz

R Main

• Mannheim

Palatinate Forest

• Nuremberg

SOUTH GERMAN HILLS

Bavarian Forest

• Stuttgart

R Danube

R Isar

BLACK FOREST

R Lech

• Munich

Ammer Lake

Chiem Lake

Lake Constance

Starnberg Lake

BAVARIAN ALPS

Zugspitze Mt

Acid rain
Many of Germany's forests, including the Black Forest, are being damaged by acid rain or have already died. Acid rain forms when sulphur dioxide and nitrogen oxides from cars, power stations and factories mix with water vapour in the air, to form weak acids. These fall with the rain. Efforts are being made to reduce the harmful gases given off by cars and factories.

Lowlands

The northern part of Germany is low and flat. It is known as the North German Plain. Rivers such as the Elbe and the Weser cross the plain. The fertile soil along the wide river valleys and in the south of the plain is heavily farmed. The area is also known for its sandy, gravelly heathlands. The most famous is Lüneburg Heath.

Coast

Germany's coastline is a popular destination for holiday-makers. The Friesian Islands in the north-west, and Rügen Island (left) in the north-east, are known for their beautiful beaches.

Forests

Germany's forests are valued for their timber and their scenic beauty. The most famous is the Schwarzwald (Black Forest). It is made up of dark fir and spruce trees, and is the setting of many German legends and folk tales.

Mountains

Germany's mountains include the Harz and Taunus ranges. The Bavarian Alps in the south contain Germany's highest mountain. The area is known for rugged scenery, such as this gorge at Neuschwan-stein, and is dotted with small lakes.

Wildlife in Germany

Wild boar, lynx, bears, wolves and deer once roamed freely all over Germany and central Europe. Their numbers were reduced through the Germans' love of hunting. Today there are still some boar and lynx in the forests and mountains. Wolves are found in East Germany. Other wild animals can be seen in nature reserves, such as Lüneberg Heath near Hamburg, and the Bavarian Forest National Park in the south.

TOWNS AND CITIES

More than 80 per cent of German people live in towns and cities. Berlin is the biggest city, with about three million inhabitants (see pages 14-15). Hamburg and Munich both have more than one million people. Next in size are Cologne, Essen, Frankfurt am Main, Dortmund, Düsseldorf, Stuttgart and Leipzig. These cities are centres of manufacturing, banking and culture. The industrial region of the River Ruhr in the west is the most densely populated area in Germany, with over eight million people.

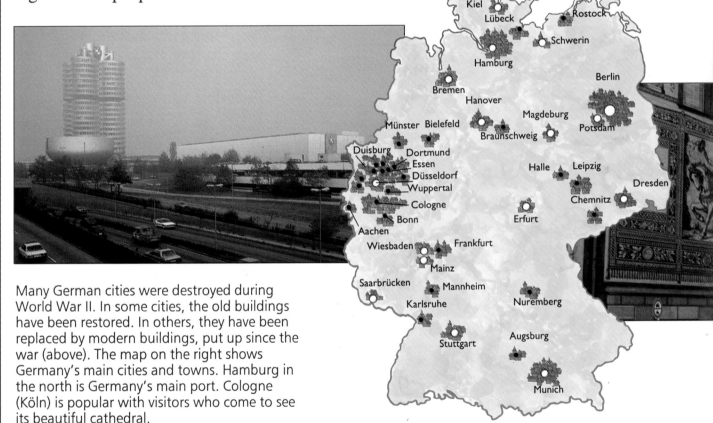

Many German cities were destroyed during World War II. In some cities, the old buildings have been restored. In others, they have been replaced by modern buildings, put up since the war (above). The map on the right shows Germany's main cities and towns. Hamburg in the north is Germany's main port. Cologne (Köln) is popular with visitors who come to see its beautiful cathedral.

Beethoven in Bonn

The city of Bonn was the birthplace of one of the world's greatest composers, Ludwig van Beethoven (1770-1827). The house where he was born is now a museum. Beethoven's hearing began to fail when he was 30, and he was deaf by 1817, but some of his most dramatic and exciting works were composed after that date.

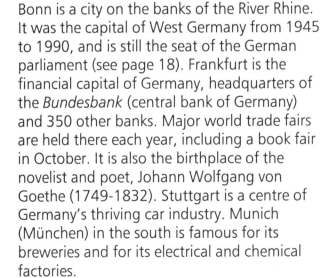

Bonn is a city on the banks of the River Rhine. It was the capital of West Germany from 1945 to 1990, and is still the seat of the German parliament (see page 18). Frankfurt is the financial capital of Germany, headquarters of the *Bundesbank* (central bank of Germany) and 350 other banks. Major world trade fairs are held there each year, including a book fair in October. It is also the birthplace of the novelist and poet, Johann Wolfgang von Goethe (1749-1832). Stuttgart is a centre of Germany's thriving car industry. Munich (München) in the south is famous for its breweries and for its electrical and chemical factories.

The Hanseatic League

The Hanseatic League was a group of powerful north German cities. The cities banded together to protect their lands and trading interests between the 13th and 17th centuries, when Germany was made up of separate states.

The League included Cologne, Dortmund, Bremen, Hamburg and Lübeck (left). These are still known as Hanseatic cities.

Before World War II, Dresden was one of Europe's most beautiful cities. Allied bombing raids devastated its historic centre, although the frieze depicting the procession of the princes, in Augustus Street, survived (above).

A place to live

Many people in German cities live in small apartments, in modern blocks like this one in Ulm, in Baden-Württemberg. Most rent their flats, as houses are very expensive to buy. There are sometimes shortages of flats and houses in cities, because so many people want to live there.

Wagner in Bayreuth

Bayreuth is a small city in Bavaria. The composer, Richard Wagner (1813-1883), lived here from 1872 to 1883, and the city is famous all over the world for its annual Wagner music festival in July. When Wagner moved to Bayreuth, he built a splendid theatre, *das Festspielhaus*, where his works could be performed in style. His famous cycle of four operas, *The Ring of the Nibelung*, was first performed here in 1876. Below is a scene from *Parsifal*, which was first performed at Bayreuth in 1882.

The Pied Piper of Hamelin

In mediaeval times, the town of Hamelin was plagued by rats. According to legend, the town was saved by a mysterious piper, who bewitched the rats with his music, and led them away to drown. But the piper was refused payment for his work. So he led the town's children away, never to be seen again.

BERLIN

Berlin was the capital of Prussia, and of Germany before its division in 1949. It is now the official capital of the new united Germany, and its largest and liveliest city. In the 1200s, Berlin was a small village on the bank of the River Spree. It grew and flourished under the Prussians, and by the 1700s was a prosperous trading centre. In the 1920s, it was one of the most important industrial and cultural cities in Europe. The Berlin Wall was built in 1961. It divided the city for 28 years, until it was demolished in 1989.

Among Berlin's most famous landmarks is the Brandenburg Gate (right), built between 1788 and 1791. It stands at the main crossing point between the east and west of the city. When the Berlin Wall was erected, the gate was stranded just inside the wall on the East German side, and members of the public were not allowed near it.

Berlin divided
In 1945 Soviet tanks entered Berlin and Germany surrendered. After World War II, Berlin was split into four zones, controlled by the Allies (right). In 1949, Berlin, like Germany itself, was divided into East and West. West Berlin was in an extraordinary position, situated deep within a hostile Communist country. Traffic wishing to pass between East and West Berlin was monitored at crossing points such as Check Point Charlie (below).

Berlin cinema
In the 1920s and 1930s many actors and writers frequented Berlin. German cinema flourished, producing stars such as the actress Marlene Dietrich, pictured below, and the director, Fritz Lang. The cinema is still important today. More than 50 nations take part in the Berlin Film Festival, held in June every year. The Festival of the Arts takes place in September.

Museums and galleries

There are over 80 museums and art galleries in Berlin. "Museum Island" lies in the River Spree, in what was East Berlin. It is the site of several museums, including the Pergamon Museum and the Bodemuseum (right), which has a large collection of Egyptian antiquities. Amongst the most precious treasures of the Pergamon Museum is a Greek altar, dating from 180 BC, from the ancient city of Pergamon in modern Turkey. German archaeologists have made many important finds, some of which are displayed in Berlin's museums.

Rebuilding Berlin

Like many capital cities, Berlin has many historic buildings and monuments, some of which have only become accessible after reunification. The *Kürfurstendamm* is Berlin's finest avenue, lined with shops, cafés, nightclubs and theatres. At its eastern end stands the *Kaiser Wilhelm Gedächtniskirche* (Kaiser Wilhelm memorial church, top left). Its ruined tower is a reminder of the horrors of war. The Charlottenburg Palace (below) was built in 1695. The monument to the philosophers Marx (left) and Engels (right), shown here, stands in a square which was used for rallies when it was part of Communist East Germany.

Crest of Berlin

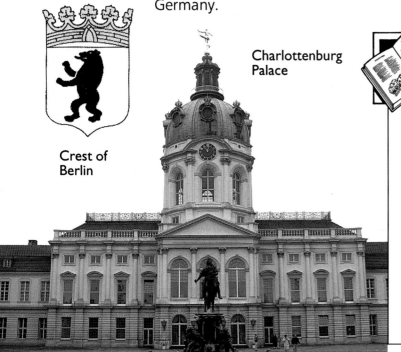

Charlottenburg Palace

Bertolt Brecht

The poet and playwright Bertolt Brecht (1898-1956) lived in East Berlin after 1949. A Communist, Brecht's plays criticised the middle-class values of the West. His most famous work was *The Threepenny Opera*. Brecht founded the theatre company, the *Berliner Ensemble*. The company toured widely in Europe. Its deliberately mannered style of acting was revolutionary and influenced many other directors.

RURAL GERMANY

Less than 20 per cent of the people of Germany live in villages. Most live and work in larger towns or cities (see pages 12-13). But there are many picturesque villages all over Germany, where people lead a more traditional way of life (below right). They include the wine-making villages along the banks of the Rhine and Mosel rivers, and the Alpine villages of the far south, with their chalet-style houses. Many villages hold a market once or twice a week. Here people can buy fresh fruit, meat and vegetables and freshly-cut flowers.

Many villages and towns along the banks of the Rhine and Mosel rivers are famous for their vineyards and wine. Two of the most famous are Rudesheim on the Rhine and Bernkastel-Kues on the Mosel, where types of German white wine are made.

The most important village landmarks are the church and the wine- or beer-tavern, the *Wein-* or *Bierstube*. Fine old buildings have survived in many villages, making them popular with holiday-makers. Many villages teem with visitors during the tourist season. At other times of the year, however, some villagers have to move elsewhere to look for work.

Architecture styles

All over Germany you will see a mixture of traditional and modern architecture. Aachen Cathedral (left) was begun by the Emperor Charlemagne in the eighth century AD, and contains his tomb. During the Middle Ages, fine cathedrals in the Romanesque and Gothic styles were built in cities such as Cologne, Ulm and Worms. The *Rathaus* in Leipzig (bottom right) served as the town hall from 1556 to 1907. In the 18th century, magnificient churches were built in the baroque and rococo styles. One of the most famous is at Wies in Bavaria. The fairy-tale castle (left) is Neuschwanstein in Bavaria. It was built in the 19th century by King Ludwig II, or Mad King Ludwig. It was used as the model for Sleeping Beauty's castle in the Walt Disney film.

Castle Neuschwan-stein

Aachen Cathedral

Old City Hall, Leipzig

Festival fun

Every region of Germany has its own wine and beer festivals. People celebrate the grape harvest or the latest wine vintage, or the first beer brewed that year. Tents are set up, where people can eat, drink, dance and be entertained by brass bands. The wreath on the right advertised the festival in Bacharach, a major wine producer. The largest beer festival is the *Oktoberfest*, in Munich.

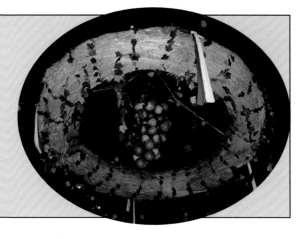

The Passion Play

Every ten years, thousands of people visit Oberammergau, a village in the Bavarian Alps, to watch the villagers perform the Passion Play. It tells the story of Christ's crucifixion, and was first performed in 1634, to ward off the Black Death. About 1,500 villagers take part in the play, which lasts over five hours. Woodcarving is a traditional village skill, and many fine religious carvings are produced.

Going to church

In the heart of every German village is the local church. There are also grand cathedrals in the towns and cities. About 45 per cent of Germans are Protestants, following the movement established by Martin Luther in the 1520s (see page 6). This movement was known as the Reformation. It spread quickly in north and central Germany, where most Protestants live today. About 40 per cent of people, mainly in the south, are Roman Catholics.

Regional costume

In many parts of Germany traditional costumes are still worn, particularly during festivals. In Bavaria in the south, the men wear *Lederhosen*, leather shorts, and the women wear lace caps and *Dirndlkleide*, (right), embroidered bodices and full skirts.

17

ORGANISATION

Germany is a federal republic, made up of individual states. In German, it is called the *Bundesrepublik Deutschland*. This was the system used by the old West Germany, which has now been adopted by the reunified country. The government is democratically elected by the people. The first all-German elections after reunification were held in 1990. Bonn is still the seat of the German government, although Berlin is now the official capital of Germany. The government may be moved to Berlin by the end of this century.

The Federal President is head of state. His rôle is largely ceremonial. The Chancellor is head of the government, and chooses the ministers of the Cabinet. Parliament is made up of two houses (see far right). The national government takes charge of national laws, defence, foreign policy and the currency.

Germany is divided into 16 states, called *Länder*. Each *Land* is responsible for its own administration and education system.

The *Palais Schaumberg* (above) in Bonn is the official residence of the Chancellor, and the site of state receptions.

The *Bundeshaus* in Bonn is home to the German parliament (*Bundestag*).

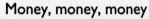

Money, money, money
The *Deutsche Mark* (DM) is the unit of currency used in Germany. It is divided into 100 smaller units, called *Pfennig*. An item worth 2 marks and 50 pfennig will be labelled DM 2,50. Germany has one of the strongest economies in the world, although it was almost ruined by World War II. The West German economy was rebuilt with the help of money from the United States, under an agreement known as the Marshall Aid Plan. Germany's quick economic recovery in the 1950s was known as the *Wirtschaftswunder*, or "economic miracle".

Chancellors
The German Chancellor is the leader of the strongest political party in the *Bundestag*. The first Chancellor of West Germany was Konrad Adenauer (1949-1963). Willy Brandt was Chancellor from 1966 to 1974. Helmut Kohl became Chancellor in 1982.

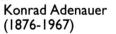

Konrad Adenauer (1876-1967)

Willy Brandt (1913-1992)

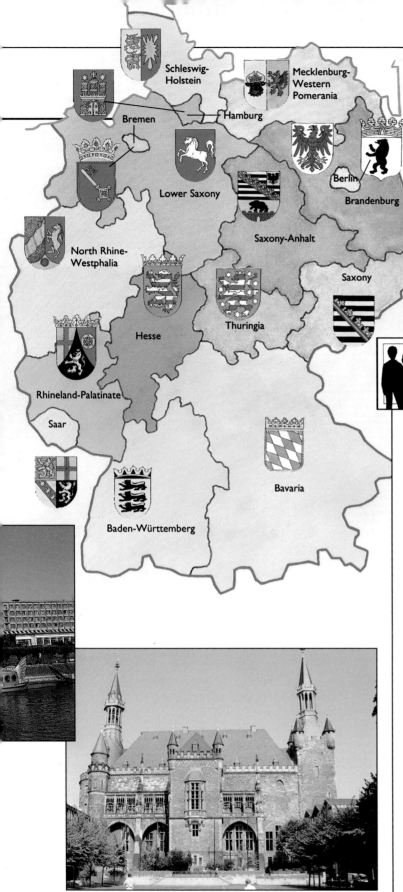

The *Länder*

The largest *Land* (state) is Bavaria and the smallest is Bremen. Each *Land* has its own state capital and regional government. Most states are headed by a prime minister, but Berlin, Bremen and Hamburg have mayors instead. Each state controls its own police force, but the states work closely together to make sure that the whole country is properly policed.

The Parliament

The German Parliament is made up of two houses – the *Bundestag* and the *Bundesrat*. The *Bundestag* is the most powerful. It has 662 members, elected for four years at a time. The *Bundesrat* represents the *Länder*. It has a maximum of 68 members. Most legislation passed by the *Bundestag* must go to the *Bundesrat* for approval before becoming law.

The two largest political parties in the *Bundestag* are the Christian Democratic Union and the Social Democratic Party. Since World War II most German governments have been made up of coalitions of more than one political party. This has tended to mean that policies have been pursued consistently. Germany's highest court is the Federal Constitutional Court, which enforces the Basic Law (the constitution of Germany).

Each German town has its *Rathaus* or town hall, where local government is administered. Many are old and beautiful buildings. This *Rathaus* is in Aachen.

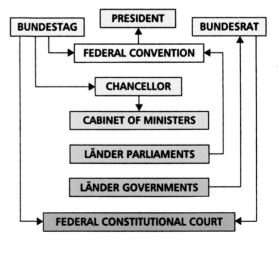

- BUNDESTAG
- PRESIDENT
- BUNDESRAT
- FEDERAL CONVENTION
- CHANCELLOR
- CABINET OF MINISTERS
- LÄNDER PARLIAMENTS
- LÄNDER GOVERNMENTS
- FEDERAL CONSTITUTIONAL COURT

EDUCATION AND LEISURE

Education, sport and leisure are very important parts of German life. School is compulsory for children aged between six and sixteen. Many stay on at school after sixteen, to prepare for university. Football and tennis are the most popular sports in Germany, together with athletics, cycling, sailing and skiing. In their free time, German people enjoy walking and outdoor activities. German workers are legally entitled to three weeks' holiday per year. Many Germans travel abroad for their holidays, visiting sunnier places such as Greece, Spain and Italy.

Sport

Football is Germany's most popular spectator sport. The national team won the football World Cup in 1990 (above). There are famous league sides such as Bayern-Munich and Stuttgart. Tennis is another major sport. Top tennis players, such as Steffi Graf, Boris Becker and Michael Stich, are national heroes.

Education

All German children are entitled to free education, funded by the state. Young children may go to a *Kindergarten*, or nursery school. Between the ages of six and ten, children attend a *Grundschule*, or primary school. At the age of ten, they may move to a *Hauptschule* or *Realschule* for a vocational education that will train them to enter a particular profession, or to a *Gymnasium*, or high school. At a *Gymnasium*, they receive a general education which leads to the *Abitur*, the university entrance examination. There are over 60 universities in Germany, with over two million students. The oldest university is the University of Heidelberg, founded in 1386 (below). The old East Germany had a much more rigid education system than the West. It is now being reformed.

The University of Heidelberg has produced many outstanding scholars and scientists.

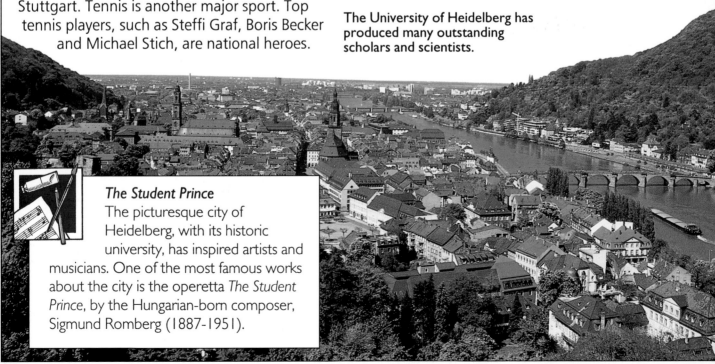

The Student Prince
The picturesque city of Heidelberg, with its historic university, has inspired artists and musicians. One of the most famous works about the city is the operetta *The Student Prince*, by the Hungarian-born composer, Sigmund Romberg (1887-1951).

Hiking
in the
Rofang
Mountains

Leisure

Many Germans are very health-conscious, and enjoy keeping fit and being outdoors. Cycling and swimming are popular activities. Many public roads have special cycle paths, where cyclists may ride in safety. German holidaymakers go skiing in the Bavarian Alps, or hiking in the forests and in the mountains (above). Networks of paths, looked after by various hiking organisations, criss-cross the countryside. They have been specially created for hikers. Sailing is another popular sport in Germany, especially at the northern city of Kiel. An international sailing regatta, called Kiel Week, is held each summer.

Join the club

About one in every three German people belong to a sports or social club, or *Verein*. There are clubs for tennis, football, shooting, swimming (below) and hiking. Football clubs outnumber all the other types of sports clubs. There are thousands of football teams, of all standards. There are also athletics clubs, which have produced many world-class athletes. East German clubs contained intensive training facilities, which resulted in many sporting victories. This tradition has been maintained. In many places, there are also youth clubs which are set up and run by the church.

Steffi Graf

Theatre trips

Germany has produced some of the world's greatest playwrights, including Goethe, Schiller, Kleist and Brecht (see page 15). Going to the theatre is very popular. There are theatres all over Germany, many of them built by German princes in the 17th and 18th centuries. There are also municipal theatres, founded by wealthy citizens in the 19th century. The German word for theatre is *Schauspielhaus*.

Johann von Goethe (1749-1832) was one of Germany's finest dramatists (see page 32).

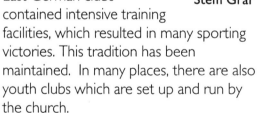

21

AGRICULTURE AND FOOD

Germany has large areas of fertile land, and a good climate for growing crops. Its farms produce about two-thirds of the country's food. The remaining third is imported from other countries. The main crops grown include potatoes, wheat, rye, sugar beet, cabbages and grapes. German wine and beer are popular, and are exported to countries all over the world. Farmers also raise pigs, poultry, sheep and cattle. Hundreds of different varieties of bread, cheese and sausage are produced. In fact, each region makes its own special type of sausage.

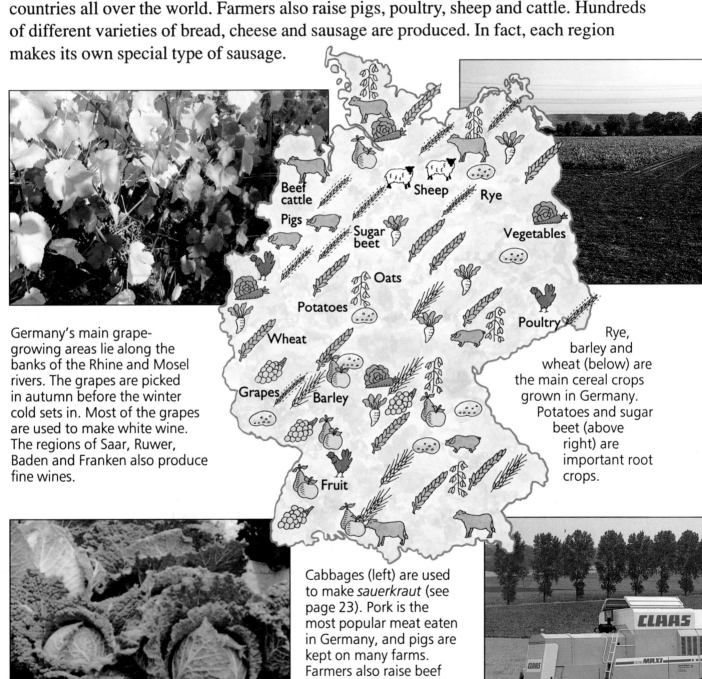

Germany's main grape-growing areas lie along the banks of the Rhine and Mosel rivers. The grapes are picked in autumn before the winter cold sets in. Most of the grapes are used to make white wine. The regions of Saar, Ruwer, Baden and Franken also produce fine wines.

Rye, barley and wheat (below) are the main cereal crops grown in Germany. Potatoes and sugar beet (above right) are important root crops.

Cabbages (left) are used to make *sauerkraut* (see page 23). Pork is the most popular meat eaten in Germany, and pigs are kept on many farms. Farmers also raise beef and dairy cattle. Schleswig-Holstein in the north is one of Germany's biggest farming areas.

22

German food

Wurst (sausage), *Sauerkraut* (pickled cabbage), Black Forest gateau, *Strudel* (pastries) and bread such as *Pumpernickel* are among the most famous types of German food. In every German town, there are snack bars (*Schnellimbissstuben*) selling sausages such as *Bierwurst* or *Bockwurst*. They usually eaten with a bread roll and a dollop of mustard.

Many world-famous German recipes were created hundreds of years ago to prevent food from spoiling. *Sauerkraut*, *Sauerbraten* (pickled meat) and sausages such as *Bratwurst* and *Frankfurters* all came about in this way.

Pretzels

German bakery

Most Germans have a breakfast of *Brötchen* (bread roll), cheese or ham, and coffee. The main meal may be eaten at lunchtime. It may consist of meat, such as pork or veal, with vegetables. In the evening, most people eat a light supper of bread, cold meats and sausages, and cheese.

Strudel

Wurst

Farms and farming

About six per cent of Germany's workers are farmers. Until reunification, farming in the two halves of Germany was carried out in very different ways. There are large farms on the plains of West Germany, but many West German farms are small and run by families. Farms are often highly mechanised, (below), although farm machinery may be jointly owned by a number of farmers. About half of the farmers have part-time jobs in industry. In East Germany, farms were much larger and were controlled by the government. They are now being split into smaller farms.

A combine harvester reaps grain in the arable lowlands of northern Germany.

Beer

Lager beer is more popular in Germany than any other country. There are breweries in many towns, and even a special law (*das Reinheitsgebot*) to protect the quality of the beer. There are about 900 breweries in Bavaria alone, producing famous brands such as Löwenbrau.

Lager is brewed from malted barley (1), water (2), hops (3), sugar (4) and yeast (5). Crushed malted barley (6) is mashed with hot water to form a sweet brown liquid called wort (7). Hops are added and the wort is boiled (8) and then cooled. Sugar and yeast are added, and the mixture ferments (9) to form lager.

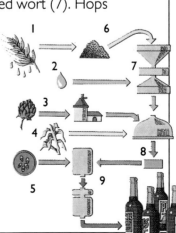

INDUSTRY AND EXPORT

Germany is the leading industrial nation in Europe. It is the world's third largest industrial producer, after the United States and Japan. Germany's industries were almost destroyed by World War II, but were quickly built up and modernised in the 1950s, thanks to hard work, and money from the United States. The *Ruhrgebiet*, along the River Ruhr, is Germany's most heavily industrialised region. It produces huge amounts of iron and steel, used in Germany's important car industry. Over 40 per cent of Germany's workers are employed in industry.

The Volkswagen factory in Wolfsburg (right) is Europe's largest car factory. The original factory produced the famous "Beetle" car in the 1930s. It was designed by Ferdinand Porsche. Compact and economical to run, the Beetle became very popular in the 1960s, and has been exported to nearly 150 countries worldwide.

Major exports

Germany trades with countries all over the world. About an eighth of all its trade is with France. Major exports include cars, electrical equipment, cement, machinery, chemicals and processed food. Many German brand names are world famous. Chemicals are made by Hoechst and Bayer. Electrical goods are manufactured by Siemens, Bosch, Braun and BASF. Precision instruments are made by Zeiss, and cameras by Leica (top left). Germany is the third largest producer of cars in the world. Famous makes include BMW, Volkswagen, Porsche, Audi, and Mercedes-Benz.

BMW launched their new "three" series in the early 1990s, as the range of cars that could be recycled. It set a trend which car makers have followed worldwide.

Daimler and Benz

The motor car was pioneered by German engineers. Karl Benz (1844-1929) made the first petrol-driven car in 1885. It had three wheels and a top speed of 11 km/h. In 1887, Gottlieb Daimler (1834-1900) built the first four-wheeled car powered by petrol engine. Mercedes-Benz remains a leading car manufacturer today.

Mercedes-Benz 280 SL, produced in 1968

Lufthansa is Germany's state airline. Many of Lufthansa's planes are supplied by Airbus, the European aircraft manufacturer in which France and Germany are leading shareholders.

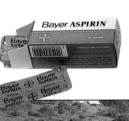

The chemical giant Bayer manufactures many kinds of medicines.

Mercedes-Benz supply heavy lorries to countries all over the world. The company is one of the largest transport equipment manufacturers in Europe.

BASF make electrical goods, including cassette and video tapes.

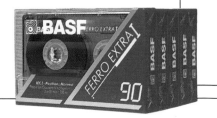

Pollution alert

In Germany, as elsewhere, there is concern about the environment. The River Ruhr is one area that has been badly polluted. The disposal of old vehicles and machinery poses a problem too. The East German manufacturer Trabant produced cars which were bad polluters. Once abandoned (see photo, left) these cars cannot be recycled; they can only be broken down using expensive chemicals.

Famous porcelain

Meissen is a small town on the banks of the River Elbe, not far from Dresden. It is famous for its fine porcelain, especially its figurines. Here, in 1708, Johann Böttger discovered a way of making European porcelain, which had previously been manufactured only in China and Japan. Meissen porcelain is marked with the symbol of crossed blue swords.

Guest workers

In the 1950s and 1960s, West German industries grew so fast that "guest workers" were invited to Germany from countries such as Turkey, Greece and Spain to fill the extra jobs created. Many of these *Gastarbeiter* settled in Germany, where they lived in poor conditions, and were not well treated. Now that there is less work, some *Gastarbeiter* have been sent back to their own countries.

RESOURCES

Germany does not have large amounts of natural resources, and must import raw materials for its industries. It does, however, have important stocks of coal (see map below) which have been vital in fuelling the massive iron and steel industry. Coal stocks are gradually running out, and Germany is turning to imported forms of energy, such as oil and gas. Germany's man-made resources include an extensive, efficient transport system. Road and rail networks in East Germany are being rebuilt to meet the same high standards as in West Germany. Canals and rivers carry passengers and goods.

Mining resources

There are important coal-mining areas in the Ruhr Valley and in Saarland in the west. The eastern part of Germany has rich supplies of brown coal, called lignite. Germany has deposits of rock salt and potash, and small amounts of uranium, copper, lead, tin, zinc and iron ore. Petroleum and natural gas are also found. Germany used to get large amounts of iron ore from Lorraine, France, when that region was part of Germany in the late 19th century. This helped industry to develop in the Ruhr Valley.

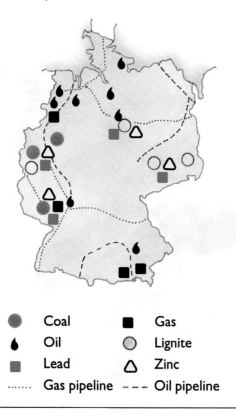

●	Coal	■	Gas
▲	Oil	◐	Lignite
■	Lead	△	Zinc
·······	Gas pipeline	---	Oil pipeline

Medicine men

German scientists have made many breakthroughs in the world of medicine. Wilhelm Röntgen (1843-1923), a physicist, discovered X-rays in 1895. He called them X-rays because they seemed so mysterious. X-rays have allowed doctors to look inside the body and investigate broken bones, lung disease and other health problems. Paul Ehrlich (1854-1915) discovered chemotherapy. This is now used to treat cancer.

Wilhelm Röntgen

The coal industry

Rich coal deposits near the River Ruhr helped German industry to grow during the 1800s. By the 1970s many of the best deposits had been exhausted. However, coal still provides much of Germany's power. The coal industry is subsidised by the German government. Stocks of coal near the surface can be recovered through open-cast mining, shown here in the Ruhr valley. The coal is burned in nearby power stations (below right) to generate electricity.

Waterways

There are many important rivers and canals in Germany. The River Rhine (below) is one of Europe's busiest waterways. The Kiel Canal links the Baltic and North Seas. It was built in 1887-1895 as a short cut for the German navy. About 100 kilometres long, it is an important ship canal.

First motorways

Germany has a network of motorways, called *autobahns*. The motorways were begun by Hitler in the 1930s, making Germany one of the first countries in the world to have them. They were intended to link Berlin with the rest of Germany. Only the United States has a larger motorway system.

Energy needs

As coal stocks fall, more oil, gas and nuclear power are being used. Most of the oil is imported from the Middle East. Hydro-electric power is generated in the south. Germany has some natural gas, but most gas is imported from Norway and the Netherlands, and from Russia, via the newly-constructed Siberian pipeline (below).

Railways

Germany has a modern and very punctual railway system, called the *Deutsche Bundesbahn*. High-speed trains run between all the major cities. There are also underground railways (the *U-Bahn*) in the major cities. Trams and trolley buses are also used.

ON THE THRESHOLD

Germany is one of the world's most influential industrial countries. Following the joyful celebrations of Reunification Day on 3 October 1990 (below), Germany faced many problems in adjusting to the union of East and West. In 1991 alone East Germany cost West Germany over US$100 billion, and it has been estimated that over the next ten years the costs of reunification could top US$775 billion. Like other nations, Germany has recently had to cope with rising unemployment and economic difficulties. However, it is a well-organised society, and will continue to play a leading rôle in European and world politics.

The cost
The costs of reunification are enormous. East German industry was old-fashioned and unprofitable. Its chemical factories polluted the environment. There are plans to spend US$155 billion on new equipment for industry, US$140 billion cleaning up pollution, and up to US$127 billion on roads and railways. These costs must be met through increased taxes, with help from the EC.

Flag of the United Nations

Germany and the UN
The United Nations (UN) is an international organisation set up after World War II to help maintain the peace and stability of its members. Both East and West Germany became full members in 1973. The united Germany is a leading member of the UN, and of the Council of Europe.

EC
The European Economic Community (now the European Community) was founded in the 1950s to promote agriculture, industry and trade through a "Common Market" in Europe. Germany is a founder member, and heads the moves toward European political and economic unity, as formulated in the Treaty of Maastricht.

Flag of the Council of Europe

The German economy
The united German economy has remained strong, though it is taking some time to adjust to reunification. The German mark is the strongest currency in Europe. The actions and decisions made by Germany's central bank, the *Deutsche Bundesbank* (right) affect the finances of many other countries. The *Deutsche Bundesbank* is an independent bank. It is based in the city of Frankfurt am Main.

International trade

Germany lies in the heart of Europe. It shares borders with nine other countries, giving it an ideal trading position. East Germany's historic links with the countries of the Soviet bloc mean that there is also great potential for trade with eastern Europe. Germany has strong trading links internationally. Some goods are exported by sea from the port of Hamburg (right).

NATO

Flag of NATO

The North Atlantic Treaty Organisation (NATO) was drawn up by the United States and several European countries in 1949. It was a military pact aimed at countering the power of the Soviet Union. West Germany joined in 1955. The Soviet Union responded by forming the Warsaw Pact, an alliance of Communist states. East Germany was a founder member. After unification Germany remained in NATO.

ESA

Germany is a member of the European Space Agency. ESA's Ariane rocket programme has begun to launch satellites for countries all over the world.

Technology

Germany continues at the forefront of technology. A good example of this is the diesel engine. Invented by Rudolf Diesel, a German engineer, in 1892, its full potential is only realised today. In the past diesel engines were noisy and slow-running. Now more efficient engines have been developed. Diesel fuel is cheaper and pollutes the environment less than petrol, so may help to lessen pollution problems.

Tourism

Germans are famous as a hardworking nation, but also for their hospitality and love of music, good food, and leisure activities. Tourism flourishes, with the development of new skiing centres, spas and health resorts. Following reunification, Germany has even more to offer in terms of scenery and historic castles and palaces, including the varied sights of reunited Berlin (below right).

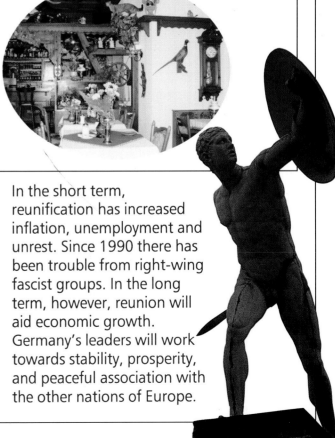

In the short term, reunification has increased inflation, unemployment and unrest. Since 1990 there has been trouble from right-wing fascist groups. In the long term, however, reunion will aid economic growth. Germany's leaders will work towards stability, prosperity, and peaceful association with the other nations of Europe.

FACTS AND FIGURES

Name: *Bundesrepublik Deutschland* (Federal Republic of Germany)

Capital and largest city: Berlin (population: 3,062,979)

National anthem: Third stanza of *Deutschland-Lied* (Song of Germany)

Official language: German

Currency: The *Deutsche Mark*;

100 *pfennig* make one *Mark*

Population: 78,700,000

Population density: 217 people per sq km (562 per sq mi)

Distribution: 16% live in rural areas, 84% live in towns

Ethnic groups: 93% German, 7% Europeans and Turks

Religion: 45% Protestant

(mainly Lutheran), 40% Roman Catholic, 2% Muslim

Area: 356,829 sq km (137,771 sq mi). Maximum east-west distance: 628 km (390 mi); north-south: 869 km (539 mi)

Highest mountain: The Zugspitze, in the Alps: 2,963 m (9,721 ft)

Largest lake: Lake Constance (Bodensee) 539 sq km

AVERAGE JANUARY TEMPERATURES

Below 24/Below -4
24-28/-4 to -2
28-32/-2 to 0
Above 32/Above 0
Degrees Fahrenheit/Celsius

AVERAGE JULY TEMPERATURES

Above 68/Above 20
64-68/18-20
60-64/16-18
Below 60/Below 16
Degrees Fahrenheit/Celsius

ANNUAL RAINFALL

More than 40/More than 100
32-40/80-100
24-32/60-80
Less than 24/Less than 60
Inches/centimetres

Longest rivers: Rhine in the west; Danube in the south; Elbe and Weser in the north; Oder in the east

Climate: Mild summers, cool winters. The Rhine Valley is the warmest area; coastal areas are usually milder than inland areas

Location: Central Europe

Physical features: The north is mainly flat, central and southern

areas are hilly; the border with Austria is mountainous

Coastline: 924 km (574 mi) on the North and Baltic Seas

Borders: With nine countries: France, Switzerland, Austria, Czechoslovakia, Poland, Denmark, the Netherlands, Belgium and Luxembourg

Forests: The Black Forest in the south-west, the Bohemian Forest

along the Czech border

AGRICULTURE

Crop production (in millions of tonnes): sugar beet 26.8; potatoes 16.8; wheat 14.1; barley 12.9; rye 4; oats 2

Fisheries (total catch in tonnes): 432,116 (1987)

Livestock: poultry 50 million; pigs 36.5 million; cattle 20.7 million; sheep 4 million

ECONOMY

One way to measure a country's wealth is to compare its Gross National Product (GNP) with other countries. The GNP is the total value of goods and services produced by a country in one year. Figures are 1990 GNPs in millions of US dollars.

USA	5,465,000
USSR (former)	2,660,000
Japan	2,115,000
Germany	1,157,000
France	874,000
Great Britain	858,000
Italy	845,000

TOP 10 IMPORTS

1. Nuclear machinery and parts
2. Transport equipment
3. Textiles
4. Electrical equipment
5. Fuels
6. Iron and steel
7. Chemical products
8. Plastics and plastic products
9. Fruit, vegetables and vegetable products
10. Food, alcohol and tobacco

TOP 10 EXPORTS

1. Nuclear machinery and parts
2. Transport equipment
3. Chemical products
4. Electrical equipment
5. Iron and steel
6. Plastics and plastic products
7. Textiles
8. Art and antiquities
9. Optical equipment and cameras
10. Wood pulp and paper

IMPORTS: (% bought from)

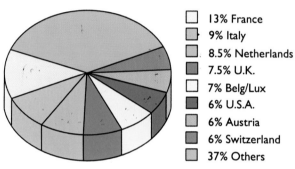

- 13% France
- 9% Italy
- 8.5% Netherlands
- 7.5% U.K.
- 7% Belg/Lux
- 6% U.S.A.
- 6% Austria
- 6% Switzerland
- 37% Others

EXPORTS (% sold to)

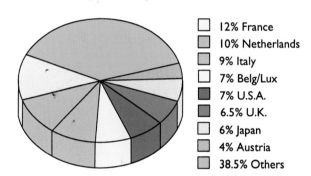

- 12% France
- 10% Netherlands
- 9% Italy
- 7% Belg/Lux
- 7% U.S.A.
- 6.5% U.K.
- 6% Japan
- 4% Austria
- 38.5% Others

INDUSTRY

Iron and steel production, manufacture of machinery, tools, transport equipment, chemicals, precision instruments

Also important:

Petrochemicals, cement, computers, textiles, ceramics, glass, food-processing

ENERGY

Oil & gas production

Petroleum 17.98 million tonnes; diesel oil 10.93 million tonnes; gas 15,871 million cubic metres (1987). The main oilfields are in Emsland, Lower Saxony.

MINERAL RESOURCES

Output in thousand tonnes (1987): Lignite 419,800; coal: 76,300; potash: 25,795; crude oil: 3,800. Small deposits of uranium, cobalt, bismuth, arsenic and antimony are mined.

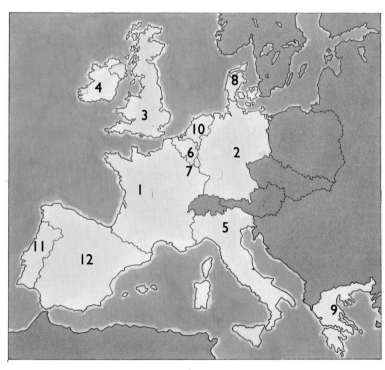

EUROPEAN COMMUNITY (EC) MEMBERS

1. France	5. Italy	9. Greece
2. Germany	6. Belgium	10. Netherlands
3. United Kingdom	7. Luxembourg	11. Portugal
4. Ireland	8. Denmark	12. Spain

FAMOUS FACES

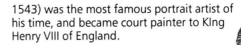

WRITERS

Johann Wolfgang von Goethe (1749-1832) poet, novelist and playwright, was Europe's most celebrated writer of the 1800s. His early writing influenced the development of German Romanticism. His most famous work, *Faust*, is the story of a man who makes a pact with the devil.

Friedrich Schiller (1759-1805, left) was one of Germany's foremost dramatists. His most well-known plays include *Wallenstein* and *Maria Stuart*.

G.W.F. Hegel (1770-1831) was a philosopher. His belief in the importance of history to the understanding of human culture has had a lasting influence on Western thought.

Jakob Grimm (1785-1863) and **Wilhelm Grimm** (1786-1859) are better known as the Brothers Grimm. They were scholars whose collections of fairy tales include Snow White and Little Red Riding Hood.

Karl Marx (1818-1883, above right) was one of the most influential philosophers of all time. The theory of Communism, practised in China and the former Soviet Union, is drawn from his most important work, *das Kapital*. Marx believed that everyone should be equal. He saw history as a struggle between rich and poor people, in which the poor would ultimately triumph through revolution.

Thomas Mann (1875-1955) was a German novelist who won the Nobel Prize for literature in 1929. Among his best known works are *The Magic Mountain*, *Death in Venice* and *Doctor Faustus*, a reworking of the Faust legend.

Bertolt Brecht (1898-1956) see page 15

ARTISTS

Albrecht Dürer (1471-1528, below) was a painter, engraver and designer of woodcuts. Dürer was an imaginative and skilful artist. One of his most famous works is the drawing "Praying Hands".

Lucas Cranach (1472-1553) was a painter, engraver and woodcut artist, best known for his full-length portraits.

Hans Holbein the Younger (1497-

1543) was the most famous portrait artist of his time, and became court painter to KIng Henry VIII of England.

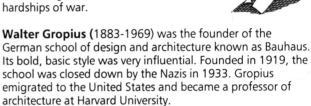

Käthe Kollwitz (1867-1945) was an innovative print-maker and sculptor. Kollwitz based herself in the slums of Berlin, and some of her greatest works champion the cause of the poor workers she lived amongst, or reflect the losses and hardships of war.

Walter Gropius (1883-1969) was the founder of the German school of design and architecture known as Bauhaus. Its bold, basic style was very influential. Founded in 1919, the school was closed down by the Nazis in 1933. Gropius emigrated to the United States and became a professor of architecture at Harvard University.

George Grosz (1893-1959) was a painter, engraver, and political cartoonist. He helped found the Berlin Dada group and invent the technique of photomontage. In 1933 he fled from the Nazi regime to the safety of the United States.

COMPOSERS

Johann Sebastian Bach (1685-1750) see page 5

George Frideric Handel (1685-1759) see page 4

Ludwig van Beethoven (1770-1827, above) was one of the world's greatest composers. He carried music forward into the Romantic period, which lasted from 1800 to 1900. His most famous symphonies are the Eroica (third), Pastorale (sixth), and ninth. Towards the end of his life, Beethoven was completely deaf, but he continued to produce moving and expressive music. See page 12.

Felix Mendelssohn (1809-1847) was a German composer, pianist and conductor. A child prodigy, Mendelssohn gave piano recitals from the age of nine. As a teenager, he was a recognised composer. He revived interest in the music of Bach, and was the most famous composer of his time.

Robert Schumann (1810-1856, above) was probably the most important composer of the Romantic movement. His most popular works are symphonies and piano compositions. In 1840 he married Clara Wieck, a brilliant pianist and a composer in her own right. Towards the end of his career, Schumann suffered from mental illness, and ended his life in an asylum.

Richard Wagner (1813-1883, right) had a great influence on European theatre and music. He built his own theatre at Bayreuth and founded Europe's oldest music festival. The most famous operas he composed are *Tannhäuser*, *Lohengrin* and *The Ring of the Nibelung*, a cycle of four works.

Johannes Brahms (1833-1897, below) was one of the greatest composers of romantic music and *Lieder* (German songs). He composed many popular symphonies and concertos.

Kurt Weill (1900-1950) was a composer best known for his music for the theatre. He collaborated with the playwright Bertolt Brecht, and composed songs for Brecht's *The Threepenny Opera*. Weill was married to the actress, Lotte Lenya. The couple left Germany when the Nazis came to power, and eventually settled in the United States.

PIONEERS

Johann Gutenberg (c. 1397-1468) see page 6

Johannes Kepler (1571-1630) was an astronomer and mathematician. Kepler discovered that the planets travel in elliptical (oval-shaped) orbits around the Sun. His theories helped the English scientist Sir Isaac Newton to understand the principles of gravity.

Gabriel Daniel Fahrenheit (1686-1736) was a physicist. He pioneered the use of mercury in thermometers, which allowed them to give more accurate readings. He also devised the temperature scale which bears his name.

Heinrich Schliemann (1822-1890) made a fortune in business, and then began a search for the ancient city of Troy, setting of the Greek epic poem, *The Iliad*. In 1871, he discovered the remains of the city, and of eight others that had stood on the same site, in northwestern Turkey.

Gottlieb Daimler (1834-1900) see page 24

Wilhelm Röntgen (1843-1923) see page 26

Robert Koch (1843-1910) was a doctor who revolutionised understanding of bacteria and infection. His discovery of the germ which causes tuberculosis won him a Nobel Prize in 1905.

Karl Benz (1844-1929) see page 24

Otto Lilienthal (1848-96) was an engineer who pioneered manned flight. In the 1890s he achieved a successful flight in a kind of hang glider – the first aircraft which could be controlled by its pilot.

Paul Ehrlich (1854-1915, above) see page 26

Max Planck (1858-1947) was a theoretical physicist who collaborated with Einstein and pioneered our modern understanding of atoms and radiation.

Ferdinand Porsche (1875-1951, above right) was an Austro-German engineer whose work influenced the development of the modern motor car. Porsche designed the Volkswagen "Beetle" and founded the Stuttgart sportscar company that bears his name.

Albert Einstein (1879-1955) was one of the greatest scientists of all time. His theory of relativity revolutionised the study of physics. In 1921 Einstein won the Nobel Prize for physics. But in 1934 the Nazis took away his German citizenship and property because he was Jewish. He fled to the United States, where he spent the rest of his life.

Hermann Staudinger (1881-1965) was a chemist whose research into polymers, a group of natural and synthetic substances which includes plastics, won him a Nobel Prize in 1953. Staudinger explained the nature of plastics, and showed how they could be made.

Hans Geiger (1882-1945, right) was a physicist who invented the Geiger counter, used to detect radioactivity. His research also increased understanding of the structure of the atom.

Wernher von Braun (1912-1977) was leader of the German missile programme which developed the V-2 rocket. This missile was used extensively during World War II, when 1,400 V-2s were fired at London. Von Braun left Germany for the United States after the war. He helped to build the first American rockets, including the Saturn V rocket, used in the Apollo Moon programme. See page 5.

German terms used in English

German and English are related languages. Both developed from a single old Germanic language, once spoken in northern and central Europe. The two languages share many identical or similar words: *Land*/land, *Buch*/book, *Sonne*/sun, *Schnee*/snow, *Maus*/mouse, *Wolle*/wool and so on.

There are a number of English words taken directly from German ones:

angst anxiety
dachshund short-legged breed of dog
dopplegänger ghostly double
ersatz artificial
flak fire (originally anti-aircraft fire)
gesundheit! bless you!
kaput broken, useless
kindergarten nursery school
kitsch in bad taste
putsch attempt at revolution
reich empire
rottweiler powerful breed of dog, from southern Germany
rucksack hiker's bag worn strapped over the shoulders
schmaltz excessive sentimentality

INDEX

Photocredits
Abbreviations: T (top), M (middle), B (bottom), L (left), R (right). All the pictures in this book are by Charles de Vere apart from: Front cover B L & R, back cover T L, title page & pages 23 T L & B line, 25 M T & 26 T: Roger Vlitos; back cover T R: Planet Earth Pictures; back cover M & pages 3 T, 10-11 B, 11 T & M L, 13 T L, 17 M, 19 L, 20 B, 21 T & 26 M: Spectrum Colour Library; 5 B L & R, 14 B R , 20 M, 21 B R & 28 M: Frank Spooner Pictures; 8 M & B, 8-9 & 9 T: Hulton Deutsch; 11 M R, 13 M & 19 R: Andrew Cox; 12 B & 25 M L : BMW; 13 T R & 14 B L: Eye Ubiquitous; 13 B & 29 B L: Mary Evans Picture Library; 18 M: The Embassy of the Federal Republic of Germany, London; 21 M & 28 B: Robert Harding Picture Library; 22 B R: Claas UK; 24 T L both: Leica Cameras; 24 M L: Volkswagen A G; 24 M R: Lufthansa-Bilarchiv; 24 B: BASF; 27 B L: RIA Novosti